Thurgood Marshall

Supreme Court Justice

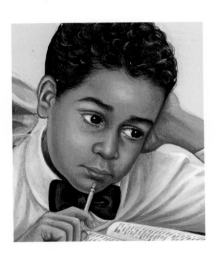

Written by Garnet Nelson Jackson
Illustrated by Higgins Bond

MODERN CURRICULUM PRESS

Program Reviewers

Leila Eames, Coordinator of Instruction,
 Chapter 1
 New Orleans Public Schools
 New Orleans, Louisiana

Stephanie Mahan, Teacher
 Bethune Elementary School
 San Diego, California

Thomasina M. Portis, Director
 Multicultural/Values Education
 District of Columbia
 Public Schools
 Washington, D.C.

MODERN CURRICULUM PRESS

13900 Prospect Road, Cleveland, Ohio 44136

A Paramount Publishing Company

ISBN 0-8136-5237-5 (Reinforced Binding)   0-8136-5243-X (Paperback)

Library of Congress Catalog Card Number: 93-79425

Dear Readers,

As a young boy, Thurgood Marshall realized that he could speak well. When he grew up, he made good use of this skill.

As a lawyer and then a judge, he helped poor African American people win their cases in the courts of law.

Read to find out the many ways Thurgood used his gift of speaking to change unfair laws and to help all Americans.

Like Thurgood, we too should speak out to stop unfairness.

Your friend,

Garnet Jackson

"Thurgood, not again!" the teacher said. It seemed that Thurgood Marshall was smart but was always getting into mischief.

1

Almost every day Thurgood was in trouble. Almost every day he got this punishment.

"Go to the basement, young man. Read a part of the Constitution of the United States. And don't come back until you can say it from memory!"

By the time Thurgood finished school, he knew the Constitution by heart.

Thurgood's great-grandfather was from
the Congo in Africa. He was brought to
America to work as a slave. But he was
so proud and strong-willed that his
owner could not make him obey.
Finally he was set free.

Thurgood's mother, Norma, was a teacher at his school. She often talked to her son about misbehaving. But Thurgood, like his grandfather, had a mind of his own.

Thurgood's father, Will, had always taught Thurgood and Aubrey to speak up for themselves. On many evenings at their home in Baltimore, Maryland, Will would sit with his boys to talk. He taught his sons to give reasons and proof for everything they said.

Sometimes Thurgood talked with his father about the Constitution. It promised equal rights to all people. But what about African Americans? Will Marshall knew that, fifty years after slavery had ended, African Americans still did not have equal rights.

This idea stayed in Thurgood's mind. Thurgood believed that African Americans needed someone to help them get equal rights promised by the laws of the Constitution.

Thurgood started college at Lincoln University in 1925. He planned to become a dentist.

While at college, Thurgood joined the debating team. Because he stated his opinions and reasons well, his team almost always won.

Thurgood realized how much he liked
winning an argument. So he decided
to become a lawyer. He would argue
for the rights of African Americans.

In college, Thurgood fell in love with Vivian Burey, nicknamed Buster. The two students married in 1928. During his last year in college, Thurgood studied harder than ever.

After Thurgood graduated, he began law school and held a job too. His days and nights were filled with work and study. When he graduated from Howard University Law School in 1933, Thurgood was one of the top students in his class.

Thurgood then opened a law office in
Baltimore and helped many African
Americans. He became known as the
poor people's lawyer. Many of the
people he worked for did not have
money to pay him, but Thurgood
helped them anyway.

The National Association for the
Advancement of Colored People—the
NAACP—asked Thurgood to work for it.
Soon he was the group's chief lawyer. He
traveled all over the country to argue for
the rights of African Americans. He won
many important court cases.

We the People of the United States, in Order to form a more perfect Union, establish insure domestic Tranquility, provide for the common defence, promote the general Welfare, and secure the Blessings of Liberty

Article.I.

Section 1. All legislative Powers herein granted shall be vested in a Congress of United States, which of Representatives.
Section 2. The House of Representatives shall be composed of Members chosen every second Year by the People of in each State shall have the Qualifications requisite for Electors of the most numerous Branch of the State Legisl No Person shall be a Representative who shall not have attained to the O

Thurgood's most famous case was against the school board of Topeka, Kansas. In Topeka, laws said that whites and African Americans had to go to separate schools. Thurgood fought against those laws and won.

16

SUMNER
SCHOOL

17

In 1954, Thurgood spoke to the Supreme Court, the highest court in the land. He proved that African American and white children should be able to go to the same schools in every state.

The next year, Thurgood's wife, Buster, died. Later he met Cecilia Suyat, whom he married. They had two sons.

Thurgood never stopped helping people. He led the way for many African Americans in the struggle for equal rights.

In 1967, Thurgood accepted his greatest job of all. President Lyndon Johnson asked him to be a judge on the Supreme Court.

21

Thurgood Marshall served on the
Supreme Court until 1991. He died in
1993. He gave his decision on many,
many cases. Each time, he remembered
what he had learned as a boy. He tried
to make sure everyone had the rights
promised by the Constitution.

Glossary

Congo (käṇg′ gō) A country in Africa

Constitution (kän′ stə tōō′ shən) The highest law
in the United States

court (kôrt) A group of judges, or the room in which
the judges meet

debate (di bāt′) A contest in which two teams take
opposite sides of a question; each team uses
reason and proofs to try to show its side is
correct

judge (juj) A person who hears a law case and
decides which side is right

lawyer (lô′ yər) One trained in the law, who helps
others in problems with the law